THE EDUCATION OF
FREE MEN

Horace Mann Lecture, 1955

THE EDUCATION OF FREE MEN

BY

ERNEST O. MELBY

School of Education,
New York University

0378920

GREENWOOD PRESS, PUBLISHERS
WESTPORT, CONNECTICUT

Library of Congress Cataloging in Publication Data

Melby, Ernest Oscar, 1891–
   The education of free men.

   Reprint of the 1955 ed. published by the University of Pittsburgh Press, which was issued as the Horace Mann lecture, 1955.
     1. Melby, Ernest Oscar, 1891–   2. Education––
1945–   3. Education––Philosophy. I. Title.
II. Series: Horace Mann lecture ; 1955.
[LB875.M345 1977]   370.1   77-1248
ISBN 0-8371-9501-2

THE HORACE MANN
LECTURESHIP

To commemorate the life of Horace Mann, 1796-1859, and in recognition of his matchless services to the American Public School System, the School of Education of the University of Pittsburgh, in cooperation with the Tri-State Area School Study Council, established the Horace Mann Lectureship. The striking and varied contributions of Horace Mann must ever be kept alive and be re-emphasized in each generation. It is difficult, indeed, to assess the magnitude of Mann's educational services. Turning from the profession of law he devoted his life to the study and improvement of education. He, more than any other, can truly be called "Father of the American Public School System." His boundless energy, coupled with a brilliant and penetrating mind, focused the attention of the citizens of his era on the need for the improvement and sup-

PORT OF PUBLIC SCHOOLS. HIS SERVICES
WERE MANIFOLD. IT SHALL BE THE PUR-
POSE OF THESE LECTURES TO RE-AFFIRM
HIS FAITH IN FREE SCHOOLS AND TO CALL
TO THEIR SERVICE ALL CITIZENS OF THIS
GENERATION. IT IS VITAL THAT ALL UN-
DERSTAND THE PURPOSE AND FUNCTION
OF A FREE PUBLIC SCHOOL SYSTEM IN
AMERICAN DEMOCRACY.

THE HORACE MANN LECTURES ARE PUB-
LISHED ANNUALLY BY THE UNIVERSITY
OF PITTSBURGH PRESS.

THE EDUCATION OF
FREE MEN

VIEWED FROM the vantage point of the easy optimism of 1913 the current threats to freedom throughout the world seem utterly unbelievable. For example, a British historian writing in a *History of Freedom of Thought* published in 1913, wrote as follows:

> The struggle of reason against authority has ended in what appears now to be a decisive and permanent victory for liberty. In the most civilized and progressive countries, freedom of discussion is recognized as a fundamental.[1]

Today freedom and oppression are locked in a global struggle which justifies no easy optimism as to its outcome. Not only is aggressive Communism a constant military threat, but, too frequently, freedom has been put on the defensive to the degree that both confusion and antifreedom behavior have often appeared among democratic peoples and governments themselves. Moreover, solu-

---

[1] J. B. Bury, *A History of Freedom of Thought* (New York: Henry Holt and Co.; London: Williams and Norgate, 1913), pp. 247-248.

tions to the problems of world peace, of race relations, of government, and community life appear now to determine as never before the future of freedom. As a result the urgency and the magnitude of the educational challenges have taken on new dimensions. Accordingly, a great deal that is said and written about education has little significance, not because the writers and speakers are insincere or technically inaccurate, but because what they write and say is based upon unrealistic assumptions concerning the nature of the modern world and its problems and a corresponding underestimation of the magnitude and complexity of the educational task. Similarly, our consideration of educational problems often overlooks both the help we could get from the new media such as television and the possibilities of new types of educational organization. Finally, as educators we seem not to have sensed the educational power of our communities, and we have failed signally to mobilize our community resources. We have shortcomings in all of these directions in part at least, because we have not realized that new concepts of energy have created social and human relations changes as striking as the power of nuclear fission and fusion themselves. If education is to preserve our freedom it must take account of these changes.

It is the purpose of this discussion to set forth briefly some of the more important steps we must take if our educational challenges are to be successfully met.

I

THE IMPACT OF NEW CONCEPTS OF ENERGY

WHEN ENRICO FERMI found that a chain reaction would and did take place in a carbon pile under the stadium at the University of Chicago, his success was announced in a cryptic telegram reading, "The Italian navigator has arrived in the New World." An equally cryptic and more significant message might have been sent reading: "A new world has arrived." For in that instant a new world had come into being. The old world was about to vanish. Every human problem was now different, from industry and warfare to the conquest of disease and the improvement of human relations. Business faced different problems, government had to be different, and education confronted a profoundly changed world. An example from the business world is striking. Speaking before the Wilmington, Delaware, Rotary Club on November 18, 1954, Mr. Granville M.

Read, chief engineer for the Du Pont Company, gave a vivid and startling account of the nature of the hydrogen age and its impact on business, labor, science, and government.

. . . during the period when the A-bomb was being designed, the scientists were searching for a way to produce one that might be many times—perhaps a hundred or a thousand times —more powerful. This was known as the H-bomb concept. Information has been given out that one obstacle was the problem of obtaining the extremely high temperatures required to ignite and fuse or bring together, under certain conditions two of the higher isotopes of hydrogen. A lead was found when the A-bomb generated temperatures as high as 50 million degrees Centigrade in one and one-tenth millionths of a second.

Such temperatures in so brief a time period are difficult for the human to comprehend. As human beings, we are accustomed to a temperature span from a little below freezing—Centigrade zero—to boiling, which at sea level occurs at 100 degrees Centigrade. As for time measurements, a second elapsed when I uttered the last two words.

The nuclear physicists, however, were no longer earthbound. They had transferred their thinking to the heavens above, and were calculating how to duplicate the reactions of the stars, so as to create on earth—and make available to mankind under controlled conditions—

the same sort of energy as that generated in
vast amounts in these celestial bodies. This is
literally what is now being contemplated in
atomic fusion.

The sun's temperature, for example, is calculated to be some 20 million degrees Centigrade. It is 93 million miles from the earth. It
gives off energy by changing hydrogen to
helium at the rate of 564 million tons per second, which is approximately seven million billion times the present rate at which electric
power is generated in the United States. Seven
million billion is seven followed by 15 zeros.
Let us not overlook the sun as a source of future
energy for our descendants here below.

Some scientists by this time had calculated
that in some stars the fusion of hydrogen isotopes generated temperatures some ten times
that of the sun, and in a much shorter time. It
was reasoned that if temperatures of a very
high order could be obtained, as recorded in
the A-bomb explosion, a fusion reaction could
be produced.

So it seemed possible now to trigger a fusion
bomb with the atomic bomb. Men had explored
the energy of the sun, and by-passed it to explore the source of energy of the stars.

In summary, the A-bomb contains fissionable
products of uranium which generate temperatures some 30 million degrees Centigrade higher
than the sun. The hydrogen bomb contains fu-
sionable products similar to the stars, and produces temperatures 200 to 400 million degrees
Centigrade.[2]

Let us note what happens, as a result, in a single example in business. Speaking of the Savannah River Project, Mr. Read points out that:

...as a scientific and engineering achievement, harnessing energy like that generated in the stars is without precedent. It demonstrates what can be accomplished when science, business, and labor willingly join hands at government request for the defense of America and the free world. It reflects the complementary responsibilities of big and small business in serving our free economy — and the people of our country.

It is estimated that some 120 different skills and talents were combined into one technological effort to achieve the final design. We drew upon the scientific talent from all of Du Pont's research laboratories. We drew management, supervision and operating personnel from across the company boards. We used professional consultants in specific fields to make sure we were not missing a bet. In a word, we called on every resource and benefited from every policy established during the Du Pont Company's background of more than a century and a half of industrial growth. This was perhaps the company's greatest contribution to the Savannah River Project.

Above all the history of the Savannah River Project is convincing proof that in an expanding

2"The Savannah River Project," November 18, 1954, a special brochure published by the E. I. Du Pont de Nemours & Company, a speech by Granville M. Read, chief engineer.

world we need big institutions for the big tasks.[3]

It is a little embarrassing to have to confess that business has sensed better the impact of the new world on its problems than we have sensed the impact of this new world on the educational challenges. Had we been as alert as business we would now have before the American people an educational program of such scope and power that it would challenge our nation to put forth every effort at local, state, and national levels in order to effect a total mobilization of resources to preserve our freedoms. Instead we have witnessed attacks on education, confusion and financial inability at the local level, and national proposals of such patent inadequacy that they have failed to commend themselves either to the profession or to the thinking public.

[3]*Ibid.*

II

WE MUST HAVE A GREAT
EDUCATION

THE NUMBERS Mr. Read uses may be beyond our comprehension but they certainly give us some measure of the magnitude of the energy concepts of the modern age. And we can see plainly that the impact on business, labor, and government is to generate an all out effort, in fact to demand total mobilization of resources. No mere tinkering and adjusting of existing patterns and practices can suffice. Writing about automation, Peter Drucker says that, "to try to build an 'automatic factory' in a business that has not otherwise been 'automated' is like trying to put a 1955 Sabre jet aircraft engine into a 1913 Ford Model T."[4] When we consider our present education with a backdrop of the challenges of the atomic age we face the reverse of this analogy. For our present education

[4]Peter F. Drucker, "The Promise of Automation," *Harpers Magazine*, April 1953, p. 42.

is analogous to a 1913 Ford engine in a 1955 Sabre jet plane. It cannot give freedom the dynamism it needs to triumph in the atomic age.

In too many places, we in the educational profession have failed to sense the arrival of the new world. We operate much as we did before. We busy ourselves with methodology leaving unanswered problems of scope and objectives. Where we do come to grips with policy and program our strategy is almost always inadequate. We are like a defense command that is lost in developing tactics and short on strategy. We are Maginot Line minded. We think better school houses and better universities will save us, forgetting that no matter how good these institutions are they cannot give us education of the magnitude required.

Even within school and college education itself our plans and proposals are lacking in scope and power. We are trying to recruit teachers for our present concepts of education when we know we should have at least 50% more teachers than we now have, even though we had no growth in enrollment. If we were to plan an education for the atomic age fully adequate to its needs, we would need not 1,250,000 teachers as now — not 1,750,000 as now estimated for 1970, but 2,625,000! Other examples could be given of our failure to get our sights up as to educational need. The all important thing for us to remember is that mankind now is possessed with the capacity to destroy itself, and that man is likely to destroy himself unless he learns to discipline and control himself. It should take no master mind to decide that as a result every human problem is changed, most of all the educational problem, for only an education of a greatness and power to match the power of our weapons and sources of energy can equip mankind to make the fateful decisions upon which its survival depends.

The changes we must make in education are not minor ones—they are major. We must reassess our task, develop a new strategy, in the form of a really great education, and revise our estimates of both the scope and intensity of the work that will be required. We must stress values rather than factual knowledge, place a greater emphasis on general education, avail ourselves of new techniques, educate more people to higher levels, mobilize our resources more fully, radically change educational organization to utilize technological advances and division of labor, and develop new concepts of leadership and administration to match the dynamism of the new age brought into being by atomic fission and fusion.

III

WE MUST STRESS VALUES
RATHER THAN FACTS

OFTEN NAIVE assumptions are made to
the effect that all education is good and
that in any case it is always on the side
of freedom and human values. If we are
concerned only with the power of education, we shall not have difficulty getting
an answer; for the power of education
has been amply proved by three men
whose careers we do not admire—Hitler,
Mussolini, and Stalin. These men proved
that education can be an instrument of
social policy—in their case, an instrumentality of slavery. So we see that education has not always been on the side
of freedom. We have to conclude that it
is not just more education we need but
a particular kind of education. Our education must, in fact, stress the values we
seek. It may, of course, be argued that
schools have always taught these values.
Have not schools taught faith in people,
respect for the worth and dignity of the

individual, respect for truth and human brotherhood? How then does it happen that several times in our history many of our people have appeared to desert our tradition of freedom and respect for personality?

In the nineteen-thirties many were deceived into acceptance of the Communist fraud. Since the second world war many have appeared to fight Communism by totalitarian methods bringing our civil liberties into real hazard. One cannot review these developments without great anxiety concerning the future of our freedoms. Clearly a large proportion of our people do not understand the full meaning of our liberties. For example, we are not as a total people nearly as concerned as we should be over violations of the spirit of our freedom. Mark Ethridge of the *Louisville Courier Journal* describes the situation as follows:

I confess that the last five years have been intellectually the most distressing of my life, because I have had the feeling that somewhere along the way we have lost what Justice Holmes called "that faith in the universe not measured by our fears." My greater distress comes from the fact that with some notable exceptions, newspapers of the country have been no more alert to what was happening to the United States than nine-tenths of the other citizens. And they should have been, if they are going to possess the power they do.

I fully believe that when historians and sociologists come to study the past five years in American history they will rank what we have done to the concepts of Livingston, Mason and Jefferson along with the Yazoo frauds, the scandals of the Grant Administration, and Teapot Dome. Fortunately, the country can quickly recover from theft, bribery, or corruption; they are physical. But this period in which we have sacrificed basic freedoms to a fancied security has left wounds that will be a long time healing and scars that will not be erased. We have seen the fulfilment of the warning which Edward Livingston gave in 1789; "If we are to violate the Constitution ... the country will swarm with informers, spies, and all the odious reptile tribe that breed in the sunshine of despotic power to convey your words distorted by calumny to the secret tribunal where fear officiates as accuser and suspicion is the only evidence that is heard."

Yes, the tide of hysteria is beginning to roll back. We are beginning to regain our senses. Even the Senate Subcommittees seem to be prepared to admit that a man should be faced with his accuser — something which we had always taken for granted until Kafka made it so vivid in his "The Trial" that there could be situations in which the accused never knows what he is charged with or who his accusers are and never enters the courtroom until his case is decided.

But we have come only a little way back.
People are beginning to stick their heads up and
to counterattack. McCarthy has been censured.
But, as Robert Hutchins pointed out to the National Press Club lately, Oppenheimer and
Davies have been cleared of disloyalty but are
not working for the Government; Ladejinsky
is not with the Department of Agriculture; and
Dr. Edward Condon, faced with his tenth or
eleventh investigation, declared himself out of
the game. The poison has gone too far to be re-
called. The librarian who got fired in Oklahoma
for subscribing to *The Nation* is not working in
Oklahoma; Mrs. Mary McLeon Bethune and
Paul Hoffman have not been invited back to
make those speeches they were prevented from
making because somebody whispered Mrs. Bethune was subversive and because Paul Hoffman was sponsored by the American Civil
Liberties Union. Larry Adler and others are
not on the American stage any more. John Car-
ter Vincent still cannot get justice from the
Government.[5]

In our fear we have condoned injustice
and plainly indicated that we either did
not understand the meaning of our freedom or felt we could no longer afford it
in the current scene.

A similar situation develops with regard to juvenile delinquency and corruption in government. Schools teach hon-

[5]Mark Ethridge, "The U. S. Press is in Trouble," *The
Saturday Review*, April 30, 1955, pp. 9-10.

esty, responsibility, reverence, and many other attributes. But often we feel the results are disappointing. Even though we know that in the current international scene our moral and spiritual values are at least as important as our material and military strength, we do not act as if we believed this. In competition with materialism spiritual considerations often come off as secondary.

I cannot escape a feeling that the total structure of American education (including schools, colleges, and community agencies) is in some degree at fault for this situation. In spite of many dedicated efforts we did not succeed in teaching the full meaning of our values nor in helping children, youth, and adults to a dedicated attitude with regard to their preservation and development.

Why did not our education give our people this dedication?

For one thing, I think we have overemphasized knowledge of facts at the expense of understanding of ideas, principles, and values. Here our examination and credit system must carry some of the

blame. A real feeling about the precious-
ness of freedom probably won't help a
student in a Regents' examination, while
some facts will.

In the second place our education has
been excessively verbal. Lancelot Hog-
ben has strikingly pointed out that if we
teach people to think without acting, we
must not be surprised if later they act
without thinking. We have a disturbingly
bookish learning which somehow con-
vinces the pupil, the student that school
is one thing and life is another, that
school is impractical idealism and life a
"go-getter" materialism. Why not then
shortcuts to riches, to power, and why
not "get" all possible subversives even
though idealistic civil liberties are vio-
lated. Some outspoken foreigner is
quoted as having said, "Scratch an
American and you scratch a vigilante."
This may be an overstatement, but most
thoughtful people are concerned about
many facets of our respect for law and
order as well as our sense of responsibility. We want freedom but are not always
willing to assume its responsibilities. We

like the protection of the law but do not
hesitate to break it at least in certain
areas of our own choice.

Whatever our great public documents
say and whatever beautiful generalities
we may express, our total education, that
is, our total life somehow contrives to
teach a distorted view of the meaning of
our freedom. Our school education is too
preoccupied with the structure of government and too little with its spirit.
Economic freedom somehow obscures intellectual and cultural freedom. Our on-
going community teaches a materialism
that overshadows whatever idealism
there is in our verbal pronouncements.

Somehow our basic values are lost in
the maze of structure and specific fact.
There should be no question about these
values. There are at least four of them
that constitute the golden threads that
give meaning and power to the tapestry
of freedom. They are respect for the
worth and dignity—yes, the sacredness
of individual human beings, faith in people, respect for truth, and unselfishness
and humility in the search for it, and

love for our fellow men or human brotherhood. These values are vastly more important than some detail of structure in
our government. They must permeate
the warp and woof of our education.

Children and youth must live whatever
values we wish to teach, be they values
of honesty or of civil liberties. They must
live them in home, school, and community. This means we are in some measure
all teachers. All of us, therefore, must be
prepared for our teaching responsibilities. All education should stress the responsibility of all citizens for preserving
our moral and spiritual values and developing our heritage of freedom to higher
levels of meaning for all our people.

It is utterly baffling to me that we
teach the average citizen almost nothing
about education, its importance, how it
is supported, organized, administered,
and carried on. We teach him about mu-
nicipal, state, and federal government.
But even though education is often the
largest single public budget of the community, we do little to make the citizen
intelligent about it. No wonder problems

of educational policy often become snarled up in controversy attended by more heat than light. Very definitely the individual citizen has educational responsibilities for which schools and universities must prepare him, and schools of education should train citizens for community leadership as well as for educational administration by professionals.

If our freedom is to survive and be further strengthened by a great education, our total education must emphasize the values of freedom not only verbally but in its life. This means home life, school life, and community life. It means too that we give everyone practical experience at the community level in living the values that constitute the real meaning of freedom.

IV

WE MUST EMPHASIZE GENERAL EDUCATION

THE TECHNOLOGICAL revolution together with developments in both domestic and world affairs calls not only for more and higher levels of education but for an educational program with a different strategy based on changed assumptions. Most of our present education rests on vocational preparation objectives. This is as true of much so-called liberal arts education as of what purports to be definitely vocational preparation. Early higher liberal arts education was vocational—in the sense that it was preparation for the ministry or teaching. Often departments of English in a college disavow all utilitarian goals, yet they are really vocational in the sense that the only field for which their students at higher levels are prepared is teaching in a college. In no real sense can such extreme specialization be seen as liberal education any more than specialization in cybernetics can be viewed as liberal or general education.

At the level of skills the automation revolution is certain to outdate—in fact, render useless much of our education in skills. Those who tend the expensive and complicated machinery need powers of analysis, capacity to diagnose, to reason from partially known data, and to know what to do in new situations. Specialized skills can best be taught by industry.

New managerial skills are needed— new leadership talents. There may well be a wave of new managerial positions for which almost entirely new types of preparation will be needed. We are in the very infancy of training for management. Much of our present management training is bookkeeping and outdated management theory. Managers need understanding of human relations, economics, and community life. This is true whether we are talking about the executive vice-president of General Motors or the manager of a Howard Johnson restaurant. We need tens of thousands of such personnel. New outlets for college

trained men and women with fundamental preparation in the social sciences
are here provided.

Nowhere in the world are fact learning and specificity as characteristic of
education as in America. We took literally the adage, "knowledge is power." We
know more than any people on earth. But
has our knowledge really given us an
education? Robert Redfield put it this
way:

Education is of course learning something,
more importantly it is becoming something. Al-
though knowledge is needed for education, an
educated person is not the same as a man who
has knowledge. An educated person is one who
is at work on his enlargement. — A person is
something it takes time to make; there is on
every such person an invisible sign, "Work in
Progress"; and the considered effort to get
along with the work is education.[6]

Our problem in achieving a more effective general education is thus in large
part a problem of coming to understand
what is meant by education. There is a
difference between teaching — meaning
the facilitation of education — and in-

[6]Robert Redfield, *Educational Experience* (Pasadena: Fund
for Adult Education, 1955).

struction. As indicated by Redfield we should measure teaching by what people are and are in the process of becoming while we measure instruction in terms of what people know. The difficulty is that our conventional measures tell us chiefly what people know and little if anything about what they are or are becoming. In my view we shall not be likely to solve this problem in school education or on the campus with verbal means. We cannot tell much about what people are unless we can observe their behavior, and if we are to observe their behavior we must observe it in real life situations. This means work experience, internship, and community participation. It means that schools and universities must have laboratories and our communities must become such laboratories. Therefore developing effective education is in large part a problem of making better use of our community resources. But more about this later.

Specialized vocational preparation will not only fail us in industry but it will not give us the kind of citizens demanded

by the atomic age. We need citizens who
want to think and who know how to
think. In no other way can freedom be
preserved. Therefore we can readily see
that general education must be our program. But achieving such education will
be a huge undertaking. At all levels of
education there must be great changes.
We need understanding rather than fact
learning, depth of insight more than narrow skills, imagination far more than
capacity and inclination to conform, and
character rather than erudition.

To get such general education a new
teacher education will be necessary. For
teachers, whose own preparation has
been a narrow subject matter or technical preparation, will not be likely to be
effective in a new education which stress-
es becoming rather than knowing.

Perhaps teacher education is as good
an example as any of the problems we
face in achieving a balance between narrow vocationalism and general education. For in teacher education the demands of the subject matter specialist
have become so elaborate, specific, and

time consuming that time does not remain to give the student the general culture, the broad social insight, the knowledge of the human organism, and human behavior that are requisite in the preparation of a teacher. In the professional education courses proliferation has followed similar proliferation in the specialties. In both areas we should reduce both the number and variety of courses.

But it is not only a mattter of the number of courses or their content. It is our attitude toward them. By some process we have convinced ourselves it is courses that educate, when we should know that people educate themselves, that it's not the courses so much that help them in this process but people. Far-reaching improvement in college education could be achieved by reducing the number of courses, as well as the number of hours in class, and increasing the opportunities for independent study, conferences with faculty, community participation.

Changes must also take place in the preparation of college teachers to make such education possible. The narrow

specialist will often be annoyed by conferences with students. Frequently, too,
he will himself lack the new well-rounded
education, the very general education we
want him to help students acquire. Here
is a vast undertaking for joint effort
between schools of education and grad-
uate schools.

Some will object that general education is beyond the capacity of many of
our people while skills in mechanical and
practical arts seem to be within the capacity of large numbers. This is a fal-
lacious and dangerous assumption, one
that has underlain many educational
policies and limited many children and
youth. It is an assumption which under-
lies many of the two-track educational
systems of Europe. It is also a dangerous
escape mechanism. If we find it hard to
interest a student in science or litera-
ture, the easiest thing in the world is
to put him in shops.

As a person with years of experience
in high school teaching, I believe general
education can be successfully provided
for far larger proportions of children

and young people as well as adults than is commonly assumed. What is more, we must do it. Our country, world freedom, will not survive without it. People of even fairly low IQ's can be taught to think. They can be helped to appreciate good music and other beauties in life. They can be helped to become informed, responsible citizens. It's hard work. It takes great sympathy, understanding, and teaching competence but it can and must be done. For these masses of people of limited ability will be parents, citizens with votes as important as those of the gifted. And what is more they have a right to the riches of human culture, and we have no right to condemn them to a narrow life by being defeatist and too readily committing them to a narrow skill education.

V

WE MUST USE ALL THE NEW
TECHNIQUES

IT IS DIFFICULT to understand the slow-
ness of education to adapt radio and television to its use. Had the medical profession made no more use of modern techniques than has education, death rates
and incidence of illness would be vastly
higher than they are. Medicine seems
constantly to seek new methods—while
in education we seem reluctant to utilize
any new technique until others have
proved its power and, in some cases, almost monopolized its use. It would appear that many in our profession still
fail to sense the power of television and
radio in education.

Radio and television have three pri-
mary implications for us in education.
They have made and are literally remak-
ing the world in which we function, they
are a powerful medium for mass education, and they can improve school education and extend its scope and power.

Because of radio and television we deal with a different public. Our public is better informed. It is under manifold influences we do not control. Its attention is taken by media more engaging than any we in education traditionally use. The new media are creating a mass mind with which we in education must deal both in teaching and in educational policy determination. If radio and television are controlled by those who oppose education, then education is in difficulty, if by our supporters, we have a great asset.

Perhaps our fundamental mistake in education with reference to radio-television has been our feeling that we could not get an audience unless we were as entertaining as commercial programs. Since we tried to be entertaining we failed often to be educational. Had we frankly set out to use radio and television for educational purposes we would have done better. Our creative power could then have been put on educational use of the media rather than on being entertaining. Also we would more likely have experimented more with the use of radio and television within schools and colleges themselves.

How many teachers can read poetry well? With television the few who can read well can make poetry live for thousands of individual children and young people. Dramatization has a power possessed by no lecture, by no page in a book. Here television is our answer. The best dramatizations can be brought simultaneously to hundreds. We can not only reach more people—we can reach them with more power and dynamism.

We confront an unsolved teacher shortage. No one seems to know how it is to be met. As of the present moment it appears that thousands of children will go unschooled or go in double sessions or be taught by inferior teachers when the teacher shortage reaches its maximum level. Certainly we owe the public and our profession a careful exploration of the use of television in this emergency. Let us admit that we do not know how far television can help us with that emergency. But we will never know till we try, till we seriously experiment with its use. If as a profession we fail to explore the possibilities of educational television, we shall be delinquent in a professional responsibility. Some foundation might well put substantial funds into such experimentation.

We know that much of what television and radio now bring to the public is of doubtful value. Much of it is plainly not educational in any desirable sense. On other cases it is influential in derogatory directions. It is of the utmost importance that teachers and administrators be aware of these media, how they operate, how they are controlled, and how they influence the life and attitude of the community.

It is no doubt true that an individual teacher or administrator may find it hard to influence a television or radio station. But such stations are sensitive to community attitude, and if educational people work intelligently with the man media and with their communities they can do much to influence the communication industries in desirable directions.

Finally we need stations licensed primarily for educational purposes, operated by school systems, universities, or groups of institutions. If full use is to be made of television in education we must have time on the air and facilities we can control. Here we must face the magnitude of our educational task squarely. Survival depends on a better informed and wiser citizenry. We cannot wait for the slow processes of formal schools and personal education. We must reach millions and reach them promptly. The mass media are one answer.

We cannot truly be said to have a great education if the mass media are either not employed or used in undesirable ways. So powerful an educational tool must not be overlooked or unintelligently employed. It is time we as educators took off our blinders in this field. It is even possible that failure to do so may be the undoing of free civilization.

VI

WE MUST GIVE TEACHERS THE AID OF TECHNOLOGICAL ADVANCEMENTS

No PROFESSION has benefited as little from technological progress as teaching. Within every other profession division of labor and technical devices are brought to the aid of the practitioner. A notable example is medicine where the highly educated physician is aided by secretaries, nurses, X-ray technicians, bacteriologists, and anesthetists. The effect of all this is to multiply the practitioner's faculties, to give him additional hands, eyes, and ears. This plan of organization increases the amount of work the practitioner can do in a day. It frees him from harassing detail and makes his day of work less exhausting. In addition he works with the constant availability of records, measurements, and other scientific data.

Contrast the situation of the teacher with that of the medical practitioner.

She has no secretary; she must type her own letters, duplicate any material she wishes to distribute. Any testing to be done is her own direct work—so is scoring of tests, recording, and record-keeping of all kinds. She has no office where she can confer with pupils or parents in confidential fashion. In so far as science has affected the teacher it has increased testing, record-keeping, and detailed clerical work so that the teacher has more and not less detail to handle. No wonder the teacher is tired at the end of the day; no wonder we make haste slowly in adopting new methods!

Why is all this? In part it is due to the economic cheapness of the teacher. Certainly in the past it would often have been hard to find any one who could help the teacher with detail who cost less than the teacher. The janitor would often cost more; the secretary as much. If teachers cost us $10,000 or $15,000 per year we would soon begin to increase their effectiveness and spread their professional skill over more pupils. But equally important is the traditional con-

servatism of the school man, his tendency
to revere the past, to live in an ivory
tower, to see educational institutions as
primarily concerned with their own self
perpetuation.

If we could throw off the shackles of
the past, we could do many things.
Where we now employ ten teachers cost-
ing us $40,000, we could employ one out-
standing creative leader at $10,000, two
at $8,000, two beginners at $3,000, two
secretaries at $2,500 each, and six in-
terns who would receive training and a
token compensation of $500. The exact
numbers and compensations are unim-
portant. The point is we should use our
money to secure and to liberate trained
intelligence, and we would as a school
system assume our proper responsibility
for the preparation of teachers. Of
course, the amount with which we
started, $40,000, is too small. The ten
teachers are too few. But, in addition,
even the ones we have are kept from becoming all they could become by a wasteful deadening pattern of organization.

Talk of teacher shortage is heard

everywhere. We have too few teachers, but the worst part of it is, we have too few really good ones. The greatest shortage is in creative minds and warm, rich personalities. In the competition for the ablest people we are not holding our own with business and engineering let alone medicine and law. One of the major reasons is we have organized education on the basis of a dead level of mediocrity. If we except administrators and a small number of university specialists, teachers begin their work at about $3,000 a year and on a national average cannot expect to earn much more than $4,500. They are all assumed to be equally competent (except for length of experience). They all do everything from cutting paper to diagnosing complex learning difficulties. The only way they can extricate themselves from the routine and salary ceiling is to become administrators or supervisors, positions which are open to a very few at best.

The effect of the system is to discourage energetic and ambitious persons from becoming teachers. Equally important the system deprives children of immediate contact with highly competent educators. There are some in most school systems but they are too far away to do individual children much good, or they are concentrating their attention on their own roomful of pupils and barred from contact with hundreds of others who need their talents badly. Every child is entitled to the best skill and competence available in his efforts to educate himself. Our educational organization should make this possible.

Often educators object to the use of division of labor and technological aids in education on the ground that the really important element in education is personal, and that division of labor removes the personal touch in teaching. They are right about the power of the personal, but they are wrong in holding to the existing pattern as a way of insuring personal attention to pupils. The net effect of our present plan is to burden teachers so heavily with mechanical detail they have little time and perhaps less vitality to give in individual counseling.

Much of our school program is of such a character that careful classification of pupils is not important. Poetry could be read by artists to high school juniors and seniors in large groups filling auditoriums. Classes in music and art appreciation can be very large. Television could be used to teach many things successfully now taught expensively and not too effectively by individual teachers in person with small groups.

We need the help of technology in meeting the teacher shortage. But we need it equally as much in our struggle to make a real profession out of teaching and in our efforts to give teaching effectiveness a new dimension. The public has a right to expect us to experiment with all these things to the end that education becomes as scientific, as effective, and as adequate in scope as possible. Until we have given teachers the benefit of every scientific and technological aid we have not placed them in a position to give us a really great education.

VII

We Must Educate More People to Higher Levels

At various times in our history we have misread the signs of social and economic change in terms of their probable effect on our need for educated people. Even experts have feared the day when we would have an over supply of engineers, doctors, lawyers, and specialists in every field. Such theorists have predicted dire social maladjustments as highly educated people would be forced by supply and demand to work at occupations beneath their educational attainments. These theorists were in one serious error: they assumed the society of the future would be like that of the present. They failed to see that technology produces demands for higher skill. Drucker points out that, "mass production upgraded the unskilled laborer of yesterday into the semi-skilled machine operator of today and in the process multiplied both his productivity and his income. In just the same way automation will upgrade the semi-skilled machine operator of today into a highly skilled and knowledgeable technician multiplying his income again."

Here we have opened for us a new vista of human opportunity. Dreary, grueling work will be done by machines under the management and manipulation of highly trained technicians. Respect for personality can now become a reality—not a mere theory. As Norbert Weiner argues, automation will lead to the "human use of human beings." There will be plenty of room for the scientist, the doctor, the teacher, the intellectual. For years all of these will be in short supply for a double reason. The need for them increases due to technological change and higher levels of education. Also society is slow and wasteful in its use of its talents.

It has been estimated that of the ablest one-third of our high school graduates only one-third go to college. This means we are overlooking two-thirds of the ablest young people, to say nothing of the many promising young people in the lower two-thirds. We have a huge pool of resources to draw upon for our top intellectual pursuits. As for the total population, it too will have to be educated to far higher levels. This will be hard to take for those leaders who feel that "education for all is education for none." Their faith in humanity is so weak, their understanding and awareness of the power of education so limited that they feel all hope rests on the development of a highly favored few.

There is even some question whether the abilities of the few can be fully conserved unless it is in a setting where all are given fullest development. The more competitors we have in an athletic contest the better the top performers seem to become. Who ever heard of a football coach who held the number of applicants for his squad down so he could concentrate on a very few? Those who hold education for all is education for none are, without realizing it, believing in a controlled economy, a controlled society, and a controlled education. They really

do not believe in free enterprise. They
also accept the concept of "scarcity economics" and "spreading" the work. The
more thinkers we have, the more creative
our total population becomes, the better
our top scientists, artists, and states-
men will be. The basic problem is not
"spreading" work, but increasing human wants and production in a never
ending series of cycles.

But it is not only the effect of our
technology that creates a demand for
more highly educated people. Trends in
both our governmental affairs at home
and in international relations indicate
that the very life of a free society depends upon a more understanding and
responsible citizenry. In recent years
there have been many signs that large
numbers of our people and of our political leaders fail to understand the full
meaning of our way of life and even the
proper relation of the branches of our
government. In most free societies the
legislative branches of the government
are on a rampage. They can not themselves govern a country, yet they will not

let the executive branch govern. Witness the case of the Bricker amendment. Moreover, it takes too long at present for our total population to become aware of a problem and to comprehend its solution. Two things are required— people must know more about the problems and must be more willing to let the executive lead using his skill, understanding, and leadership before it is too late. Both require a higher level of education on the part of both the masses of people and leadership. Our government is intended by our Constitution to be representative. Congressmen are not assumed to be mere mouthpieces for a Gallup poll of the citizens. We should expect them to use their expert knowledge, their best judgment even at times when a temporary wave of popular opinion (due perhaps to lack of full information) may run in a counter direction. We do not or should not want our representatives in Congress to follow every pressure group or every demagogic blast in press or radio. Yet because so many of us misunderstand our governmental theory and structure there is some doubt as Walter Lippmann puts it, "that both liberty and democracy can be preserved before one destroys the other."[7] Lippmann's plea for the development of a public philosophy is most assuredly timely. But we shall not make the public philosophy effective without an education of vastly greater power than the one we have at present.

For one thing the proportion of adults in society is growing. Adult education is paramount. This is true, not only because the adults control our society, but also because their influence on the children and youth is so powerful schools and colleges can do little without support from homes, churches, mass media, and community life generally.

One problem alone facing the modern world seems clearly to defy solution except through better and more widespread education. I refer to the problem of attaining world peace through more effective universal law and order. The problems here are involved and little un-

[7]Walter Lippmann, *The Public Philosophy* (Boston: Little Brown and Company, 1922), p. 13.

derstood by the general public. We be-
moan loss of sovereignty to the United
Nations, but we ignore the loss of sovereignty that we inevitably suffer in a
war torn world. We seem to forget that
sovereignty will mean little if humanity
is destroyed. There are so many things
we must learn, such as the importance of
having allies and of communicating with
them, the necessity of knowing something about other cultures and peoples
if we are to get along with them, and the
mistakes we make in seeking to determine the governmental patterns of other
countries. Every school from elementary
grades to college and every adult educat-
ing agency should seek to equip people
for making intelligent choices in foreign
policy. No matter what extremists may
say we are world citizens and the more
responsible and intelligent we are as
world citizens the more devoted and dedicated is our American citizenship.

But it is not only at the national and
international levels that we need higher
attainments in education. Changes are
taking place in the community that em-

phasize the need for capacity for leadership on the part of all of our citizens. Much of this preparation cannot be secured from book study but must be learned in practice at the community level. Colleges must institute far more learning by doing, high schools must develop programs of work experience, and all education must take on a new vitality and concern with life .

The current reaction against universal education is dangerous. Even well-known authorities have advocated the lowering of compulsory school attendance laws on the ground that schools have not learned how to deal with the children of non-verbal abilities. This is a dangerous escape mechanism for schools which should be challenged with the task of building an education which meets the needs of such young people rather than take the easy way out of letting them leave school. Were a similar policy to be followed in a hospital it would dismiss its critically ill patients rather than work hard to bring them back to health. Much more could be done for children of lower abilities —

in fact, much is now being done. These methods and programs need extension.

VIII

WE MUST MOBILIZE ALL OUR RESOURCES

NEARLY ALL of our work in formal school education has been based on the assumption that we could so influence children and youth in our schools, that they in turn would improve our society. This assumption underestimates the size of our task, misunderstands its nature, exaggerates the power of schools, and fails to take account of the power of communities in education. Because we have claimed too much for what we could do in school houses, the public has blamed us unjustly and has also been less inclined to help, since it may in some instances have been given the feeling we did not need or want its help.

The tempo of social and technological change and a lengthened life span have changed the role of schools and formal education emphasizing the need for adult and informal education. Changes take place so rapidly in the current scene that schooling can not hope to give the individual education that will equip him for the entire span of his life. In fact, much of what he learns in high school will be outdated when he receives his college diploma. In addition the tempo of social change is increasing so this situation will be worse in the future and not better. A recognition of these conditions should tell us to emphasize the general rather than the specific, principles rather than facts, how to think rather than what to think.

But no matter how well we succeed in formal education in such directions, continuous education is essential. In reality, of course, we have lifelong education now, for communities always educate. The only questions are, in what way, for what ends, and how effectively. We know that radio, television, and the printed page have radically increased the power of community agencies over the thinking, attitude, and behavior of the individual. Our problem is how to influence the power of the community in desirable directions.

Here we are up against two hard re-
alities. We need all the resources of the
community because our challenge is so
great we cannot meet it without their
fullest use. Equally important, we can
not mobilize these resources by mandate.
We do not have the control and even if
we had it, we could not use it and remain
a democracy. Baffling as our situation
seems, it is by no means hopeless. In fact,
it may well be at this point that our faith
in freedom receives its hardest test. For
if we can make common cause with the
people and the agencies of our communities, we can help these communities to
become educational enterprises in the en-
tirety of their functioning. This would
mean that all community processes—
even those in private business and voluntary association take on educational purposes. In other words, our solution is a
community fully mobilized for education.

Now we must take a hard look at ourselves. We cannot produce the fully mobilized community unless we become *one*
of the educational agencies of the community rather than insist that we are

the agency for education. We must stop
trying to dominate the community, stop
trying or hoping to direct all education,
and humbly take our place as members of
the community as it organizes itself for
educational purposes.

I know full well how many fears I
evoke by this statement. Have we not
suffered, you will say, from too much
community control? No, we have suffered at the hands of minorities, busy-
bodies, and good people who could not
see their proper role. We have suffered
too because only the destructive minorities were organized and the community
as a whole had no channel through which
it could make itself felt. We must give
majority opinion media for expression
at least as effective as those taken by
minorities in their often militant and destructive efforts. Some kind of a community council is necessary. It should
be representative in character, that is,
it should include persons from a cross-
section of the various interests of the
community. It should be a free forum
for the discussion of matters of social

and educational policy. To the degree
that it is such a forum it can be a great
help to the board of education and school
administration in determining educational policy.

Strange as it may seem we shall gain
and not lose strength in community mobilization. Here is a prime example of
the Biblical statement, "He who loses
his life shall find it." For no one can educate anyone else. People educate themselves. And if we can help people to find
ways of doing things for themselves and
their communities, we can set in motion
an educative process of such power that
it dwarfs schools and colleges in magnitude. This does not mean that schools
and colleges lose importance — they
merely change their role and their relationship to the community. As they relate themselves to their communities,
they serve the community, but the community also serves them. It becomes a
laboratory in human living for the faculty and students.

Our colleges and universities spend
millions for laboratories in physical sci-

ence. By comparison we are singularly lacking in laboratories on campus in the social sciences and the humanities. But nearly all such colleges are located in communities. Within a few minutes ride can often be found every facet of modern life. Moreover, our communities have been suffering from fragmentation. The cement that once held them together is breaking apart at the seams. They have great resources but they need the professional assistance of our university faculty members.

We see here how university education for our students and community leadership can vitalize one another. Also work in the community will give a new vitality to the college faculty member. If university faculty members work together on community projects, they will overcome the semantic obstacles which now separate them into compartments.

But the greatest reason for using our community resources is that, when education takes place as a result of participation in the community, it overcomes its bookish character and takes on a new effectiveness. We have already noted that education is more than fact learning—it is a process of becoming, and the "becoming" process takes place largely as a result of what people live. This is as true for the people of the community as it is for the students who use that community as a laboratory. Thus, if educational institutions can effectively relate themselves to communities, we shall develop the most effective type of adult education in addition to giving new vitality to the preparation of our youth for citizenship.

It may well be that we should adopt the suggestion of Dean Rosecrance of New York University that teachers divide their day or week between teaching children and youth in school and work with adults in the community. Think how vital and interesting the teacher would be were she to come to her school room direct from facing community problems. And her work with children and youth would be helpful in facing many adult problems.

In every community there are people

of specialized talents who can make a
signal contribution to our schools and to
adult education. There are people who
have traveled, others represent the pro-
fessions, still others in the fine arts.
Then we have government officials, local,
state, and national. In a city like New
York the range and number of persons
that can be drawn upon for assistance
with the educational task are enormous.
Most of the time such citizens are glad
to participate without charge. They are
glad to help out in education and often
feel honored to be asked. We all like to
be useful. I have never seen such a citizen take part in an educational task
without noticing that he went away with
a clearer idea of the work of schools and
increased interest in the problems of education. People who have thus helped
us will be friends of education for they
have put something of themselves into
the educational enterprise.

Thus, when we use our community resources, we not only get needed resources
but we establish better communication
with our communities and bring about

better understanding of education. Here
we have the makings of what we mean
by a great education. It is an education that is all out, one that no one can
escape, one that in its on going life literally picks people up, energizes them and
involves them in an activity which is
simultaneously educational for them and
for others who participate. This is what
we mean by the fully mobilized, the education centered community.

If we are to meet the educational challenges resulting from new concepts of
energy, we must revise some of our stub-
born notions about the financing of education. The opposition to federal aid for
education is not intelligent opposition.
Senator Taft, after study of the problem, became convinced federal aid was
unavoidable if schools were to be prop-
erly supported. If we had a really great
education in this country, an education
effective enough to meet the needs of
the hydrogen age, it would cost at least
twice what our present education costs.
There is no practical way under our
political system of getting this much

money for education without federal
sharing of the cost. Eventually we will
come to federal aid. Students of the
problem have realized this for years.
Somehow we must help our people as a
whole to see the need.

In some communities our total education is weakened by an unsatisfactory
relation between public, private, and parochial schools. Unfortunately, religious
bigotry or intolerance too often enter
the discussion of this problem. It is un-
thinkable that when even the fullest cooperation and the best efforts of us all
are not likely to give us all the educational facilities we need that there
should be antagonism. We need all the
schools of America, public, private, and
parochial. We should stay in close touch
with one another, support one another
sharing our experiences and coming to
each other's defense when one or the
other is attacked. We have much to learn
from each other. No community can be
said to have made a full mobilization of
its educational resources until it has
friendly, genuinely cooperative relation-

ships among its public, private, and parochial schools.

At times the claim is made by public
school people that those who send their
children to private or parochial schools
tend to lose interest in public education.
Any parent has the right under our
American system to send his children to
a private or parochial school. But we
have a right to remind such parents, as
well as others, that there are no private
or parochial schools behind the Iron Cur-
tain and should freedom ever go down to
defeat in America there will be none
here. Therefore no one has a bigger stake
in the success of public education than
those who send their children to private
and parochial schools. Nothing they can
buy for themselves or their children will
save either them or their children from
the consequences of the public school's
failure if it does fail, and if as a result,
our freedom is lost. One's very right to
educate his children as one believes they
should be educated depends in very large
measure on effective public education.

Desegregation will give us a great new

source of trained citizens and professional competence. Once the Negro has a greater feeling of equality his potential capacities will be released to a far greater extent. Those of us in universities who work with Negroes from segregated areas have had ample opportunity to observe the creative effect of the removal of the blight of segregation. We need the creative capacities of every individual in America regardless of race. Once this hurdle has been surmounted, new creativity and productivity lie ahead.

In short, we must educate more people, and we must raise them to higher educational levels. Here is a challenge we can meet. We should at least double our present college and university enrollment, double the number we prepare annually in nearly every profession. This means sharply increased facilities for higher education with both public support and private philanthropy for higher education doubled and perhaps trebled. It has to be done. Our free society will not survive in the hydrogen age without such a program.

Building such an education, as we have just indicated, by mobilizing our total resources is a challenge that can bring us to greater unity in the community, in our states, and in the nation. It is a challenge we can meet together gathering strength and solidarity in the process.

IX

WE MUST DEVELOP A NEW CONCEPT OF LEADERSHIP AND ADMINISTRATION

BY NOW you are probably asking, "How is this great education, this vast, complex community, so rich in resources to be mobilized"? Is not (you will say) this a feat in human engineering that is beyond us? Some might even say only a dictator could achieve such full use of resources. Such a person would be quite wrong for only truly democratic leadership can possibly effect the mobilization we need. So this becomes our key problem: How can we develop a leadership and administration democratic in spirit and effective in action? Here there are many pitfalls. Democracy in administration does not mean mere teacher control —this may be only an oppressive bureaucratic collectivism. It does not mean that school administrators are mere office boys for teacher groups or for pressure groups at the community level. Delegation of responsibility is not undemocratic. Use of expert judgment is not a violation of the meaning of freedom. Our leadership must be creative, it must be dynamic, it must use the findings of research, and it must bring about the fullest use of our resources. If it is to be and do all of these things, it must be very different from our past administration. Such administration can not be produced by administrators or experts alone. It will be developed only in the crucible of experience. Teachers must help, people must take part, students of administration must participate, government must play a role of facilitation and not mere opposition as is now so often the case.

Within the profession of leadership and administration, we need a new conception of our challenge. We are too often "schoolhouse" minded. We think in too small terms. We ask for too little—fearful that if we ask for what we need we will offend. Our sights are not up, our horizons are too narrow, our ceiling for operations too low. We do not sense the power of faith and the potentials of

individual human beings. Nor do we re-
alize how rich our own lives would become if we opened our hearts to others
in love and understanding.

After more than forty years in teaching and administration, I continue to be
baffled concerning our failure to sense
the power of creative leadership. Can
anyone really teach without marveling
at the creative power of individual children and youth as their unique personalities unfold, so to speak, and present
us with new ideas and creative achievements? Can anyone administer a school
without being moved by seeing a beginning teacher respond to faith and in-
spiration, overcome obstacles, and become a creative leader? Can one see lay
people at the community level take un-
certain first steps in community organization, later to grow in security and
effectiveness, finally to emerge as glow-
ing, confident, yet humble personalities
strong because they have a feeling of
belonging with people and creative because they have sensed the power of
freedom and participation? If we have

seen them, then why do we not operate on them? Why do we not put them to immediate use?

Much of our past theory in educational administration has been borrowed from industry and military affairs. In spite of all its shortcomings in terms of educational philosophy and outdated management theory, the school board superintendent pattern of administration has great achievement to its credit in this country. American educational administration has stimulated educational growth more than has administration in any other country. Yet, even though we allow for all the victories that can be chalked up to its credit, educational administration has recently been running into rough weather. As educational programs have broadened, as community involvements have increased, and as public interest in educational policy determination has grown, the need for a fuller use of community resources has become urgent. In many instances conflicts have arisen because of lack of communication and unwise behavior on the part of professionals in their community relations.

Within educational institutions themselves, there have been marked trends in the direction of greater democratization of administration with wider faculty participation in the determination of educational policy. While growth in democratic attitudes and improved human relations have brought great improvement to the quality of our leadership, much of what has happened in faculty participation has raised as many questions as it has answered. In some instances faculty control has served to forge a chain of restriction about the individual faculty member rather than to liberate his creative talents. In part this is due to confusion in our thinking with regard to the meaning of both democracy and freedom. Clearly, if none of us can do anything unless all give permission, then none of us will have much freedom. Similarly, if each of us insists being a law unto himself, there will be little real democracy or integration in our educational programs. However, since educa-

tion is primarily creative living, freedom
for individual creative effort is a paramount consideration. Collective decision
in policy making must not be carried so
far that the individual finds himself and
his creative powers restricted. Dynamism must be preserved. Education
must have freedom of movement and a
dynamic forward thrust. Our challenge
is, therefore, to develop a concept of administration which is democratic, hu-
mane, and creative in spirit but organized so as to provide both freedom and
mobility. Such administration provides
a very definite and creative role for the
administrator and also defines roles of
teachers and others interested in the
educational enterprise.

In the past our educational administrators have not been adequately
prepared for their role as community
leaders. They have been viewed as superintendents of schools rather than as
superintendents of education which, in
fact, they must be if we are to have a
full mobilization of our community resources. New patterns of relationship

must be developed between our school administrators and leaders in voluntary associations, governmental agencies, and community groups generally. Our administrators must learn how to function as catalytic agents rather than as administrative directors who give orders. Many of these relationships must be developed in practice, and we can as yet see only the broad outline which the activities must take.

Within educational institutions themselves, we need a new dynamic power and human warmth in the conduct of our work. When we borrowed the older industrial pattern, we got the shortcomings as well as the strength of this design. Now, in order to develop a great education, we need an administrative concept with a new power and inspirational leadership far greater than any we have been able to exert in the past. Such influence will not come from mechanical arrangements, organizational diagrams, or involved administrative theory no matter how excellent these may be in themselves. We will, I am sure,

influence our associates most through our
faith in them, through our respect for
their worth and creative power, through
our integrity in the search for truth, and
in the degree to which we give our associates affection and understanding. It is
out of these qualities of human beings
and these elements of human relationships that our new and more vital educational administration must be forged.

X

THE CHALLENGE OF NEW CONCEPTS OF ENERGY

THE THERMONUCLEAR age confronts mankind with a frightening set of alternatives. This age says to man, "Change yourself or you will destroy yourself. With faith you can live, go defeatist and you will die. Recognize the sacredness of individual human beings and you can build a free and creative society, fail in this and you will forge the links of the chain of your own slavery. Seek and respect the truth and new vistas of human service and well-being are yours, prostitute the truth and the search for it to selfish ends and your freedom will be lost. Look upon all men as your brothers and a friendly world will gradually become a reality, embrace racism and chauvinistic nationalism and you see only war and destruction ahead."

Education is our instrumentality for changing human beings, for replacing bad ideas with good ideas, defeatism with faith, anti-intellectualism with the search for truth, human conflict, and antagonism with human brotherhood. To do these things it must be a great and powerful education permeated by the values which it seeks. It must further the fullest growth of men and women not only the preparation of specialists. It must avail itself of all the devices and processes brought to us by science. It must lift all men to higher levels of creative achievement. It must use our every resource and be energized by a creative, dynamic, and inspiring leadership. Can we build such an education?

As long as the atomic scientist was earthbound he could not trigger the hydrogen bomb. But when he lifted his thinking to the heavens above he found his answer. As long as we in education seek our program and processes in the practices of the past, as long as we assume the present world to be like the past, we shall arrive with what is too little and too late. But if we design our education program with the alternatives of the thermonuclear age as a backdrop

for our enterprise, we shall like business
and technology raise our sights. Such a
backdrop will enable us to make a real-
istic appraisal of our task. It will force
us to use all our resources. An accurate
estimate of the work to be done will get
before us an educational challenge so
formidable that we will be forced to use
the mass media and to organize schools
economically and efficiently. In the same
way as the Savannah River project could
not have been brought to successful
fruition without superb organization,
administration, and leadership so the
success of a truly great education rests
on our capacity to develop educational
leadership of new scope, power, and creativity. All these things we can do. But
will our education be great in the realm
of values, in the things of the spirit?
Will it put humanity first, and will it be
itself a living expression of the best
aspirations of humanity in the challeng-
ing decades ahead? This is really the
key question to our ability to develop a
great education. It is the key question in
the education of free men.

On the technological front we appear
to have met every challenge. We have
released colossal energy through fission
and fusion. We have made the industrial
and military adoptions we needed. For
one I refuse to grant that a human intelligence, which has done all of these
things, cannot also meet the moral, spiritual, and educational challenges. This
will especially be true as we increas-
ingly recognize that the price of failure
is extinction, and the reward for success
is, not only survival, but the ushering in
of a new era in human history in which
man's achievements on every front will
outdistance those we now know by the
same proportions as the temperature of
the sun exceeds that of your kitchen
stove.

There is talk of a lithium bomb. It has
been said that if all the water in the
oceans were gasoline, its power would
not equal that of one lithium bomb. Perhaps this is an exaggeration. Be that as
it may, we can be sure our measures and
concepts of energy will rise. As they do
they can frighten us to self destruction,

or they can inspire us to achieve new concepts of creative human living under freedom. Education can make the difference if its greatness, power, and spirituality match our expanding concepts of energy with their resulting challenges.